ay the sounds and blend them together to read the word. What does the mouse think?

Look at the letters and say the sounds.

or
ee
p
o
u
a
e
j
i
ie
n
oa

Say the sounds and blend them together to read the words.

Say the word *egg* and listen out for the sounds: *egg* – /e-g/.
(There is one sound dot underneath the egg for each sound in the word.)

oats

seeds

Say the word *cake* and listen out for the sounds: *cake* – /c-ai-k/.

Read the words and spot the objects in the picture.

coffee

pie

muffin
milk

melon

corn

nuts

toffee popcorn